TheLittle book of DiRTY j

Books by Boxer:
Swinnow Lane, Bramley,
Leeds, UK LS13 4BS

Tel: 01133 955 593
Fax: 01133 955 594
email: sales@booksbyboxer.com
Web: www.booksbyboxer.com

Copyright © 2008 Books by Boxer
Cover and interior layout by Sanjit Saha
Cover image courtesy of Getty Images

ISBN 9781909732063
Item Code: YLB0037

Printed and bound in China

A bloke goes into the job centre in Newcastle and sees a card advertising for a gynaecologist's assistant.

Interested he goes to learn more. "Can you give me some more details about this?" He asks the guy behind the desk.

The job centre guy sifts through his files and replies, "Uh — yes here it is... OK, the job entails you getting patients ready for the gynaecologist.

You have to help them out of their underwear, lie them down and wash their nether regions.

Then apply shaving foam and shave off all their pubic hair then rub in soothing oils so they're ready for the gynaecologist's examination.

There's an annual salary of £60,000 but I'm afraid you'll have to go to Oxford."

"Oh why, is that where the job's based?"

"No "that's where the end of the queue is"!

A guy is browsing in a pet shop and sees a parrot sitting on a little perch. It doesn't have any feet or legs.

The guy says aloud; "Jeesh. I wonder what happened to this Parrot?"

The parrot says, "I was born this way. I'm a defective parrot."

"Holy shit," the guy replies. "You actually understood and answered me!"

"I got every word," says the parrot. "I happen to be a highly intelligent, thoroughly educated bird."

"Oh yeah?", the guy asks, "Then answer this - how do you hang onto your perch without any feet?"

"Well," the parrot says, "this is very embarrassing but since you asked, I wrap my willie around this wooden bar like a little hook. You can't see it because of my feathers." "Wow" says the guy, "you really can understand and speak English, can't you!?"

5

"Actually, I speak both Spanish and English and I can converse with reasonable competence on almost any topic: politics, religion, sports, physics, philosophy. I'm especially good at ornithology. You really ought to buy me. I'd be a great companion."

The guy looks at the £200 price tag. "Sorry, but I just can't afford that."

"Psssssssst" says the parrot, "I'm defective, so the truth is, nobody wants me cause I don't have any feet. You can probably get me for £20, just make the guy an offer"

The guy offers £20 and walks out with the parrot.

Weeks go by. The parrot is sensational. He has a great sense of humour, he's interesting, he's a great pal, he understands everything, he sympathises, and he's insightful.

The guy is delighted.

One day the guy comes home from work and the parrot goes "Pssssssssssssst" and motions him over with one wing. "I don't know if I should tell you this or not, but it's about - your wife and the postman."

"What are you talking about?" asks the guy

"When the postman delivered today, your wife greeted him at the door in a sheer black nighty and kissed him passionately."

WHAT???" the guy asks incredulously. "THEN what happened?"

"Well, then the postman came into the house and lifted up her nighty and began petting her all over" reported the parrot.

"My God!" he exclaims. "Then what?"

"Then he lifted up the nighty, got down on his knees and began feeling all over her body - starting with her breasts and slowly going down...."

"WELL???" demands the frantic guy, "THEN WHAT HAPPENED?"

"Damned if I know. I got a hard-on and fell off my perch.

Three women were talking about their love lives.

The first said, "My husband is like a Rolls-Royce; smooth and sophisticated. "

The second said, "Mine is like a porsche; fast and powerful."

The third said, "Mine is like an old Morris Minor. It needs a hand start and I have to jump on while it's still going."

A man is sitting in a fancy restaurant and there is a gorgeous brunette sitting at the next table. He has been checking her out since he sat down but lacks the nerve to talk with her.

Suddenly she sneezes, and her glass eye comes flying out of it's socket toward the man. He reflexively reaches out, and grabs it out of the air, and hands it back.

"Oh my, I'm so sorry," the woman says as she pops her eye back in place.

"Let me buy you dinner to make it up to you," she says.

They enjoy a wonderful dinner together, and afterwards they go to the theatre followed by drinks. They talk, they laugh, she shares her deepest dreams and he shares his. She listens.

After paying for everything she asks him if he would like to come to her place for a nightcap and stay for breakfast. They have a wonderful, wonderful time.

The next morning, she cooks a gourmet meal with all the trimmings. The guy is amazed. Everything had been so incredible!

"You know," he said, "You are the perfect woman. Are you this nice to every guy you meet?"

"No," she replies......

She says:

"You just happened to catch my eye."

An American boards an airplane and takes his seat. As he settles in, he glances up and sees a most beautiful woman boarding the plane.

He soon realises she is heading straight towards his seat. A wave of nervous anticipation washes over him.

Lo and behold, she takes the seat right beside his.

Eager to strike up a conversation, he blurts out, "Business trip or vacation?"

"Nymphomaniac Convention in Chicago," she states.

Whoa!!! He swallows hard and is instantly crazed with excitement. Here's the most gorgeous woman he has ever seen, sitting RIGHT next to him and she's going to a meeting of nymphomaniacs!

Struggling to maintain his outward cool, he calmly asks, "What's your business role at this convention?"

"Lecturer", she says. "I use my experiences to debunk some of the popular myths about sexuality."

"Really," he says, swallowing hard, "what myths are those?"

"Well," she explains, "one popular myth is that African American men are the most well-endowed when, in fact, it is the Native American Indian who is most likely to possess that trait. Another popular myth is that French men are the best lovers, when actually it is men of Greek descent."

Suddenly, the woman becomes very embarrassed and blushes. "I'm sorry." she says, "I shouldn't be discussing this with you, I don't even know your name!".

"Tonto," the man says, as he extends his hand. "Tonto Papadopoulos."

A little old lady was going up and down the halls in a nursing home.

As she walked, she would flip up her night gown and say, Super sex! Super sex!

She walked up to an elderly man in a wheel chair. She flipped up her night gown in front of him and said, Super sex!

He sat silently for a moment or two looking up at her.

Then he finally answered,

.."I'll take the soup

A little girl asked her mother, "Mum, may I take the dog for a walk around the block?" Mum replies "No, because she is in heat." "What's that mean," asks the child."

"Go ask your father" Mum replied, "I think he's in the garage." The little girl goes to the garage and says, "Dad, may I take Belle for a walk around the block? I asked Mum but she said the dog was in heat and to ask you."

Dad said, "Bring Belle over here." He took a rag, soaked it in petrol and scrubbed the dog's backside with it and said, "Okay, you can go now, but keep Belle on the leash and only go around the block." The little girl left and returned a few minutes later with no dog on the leash. Surprised Dad asked, "Where's Belle? The little girl said, "She ran out of gas about halfway around the block, so another dog is pushing her home."

Mr.. Smith hired a beautiful secretary. She was young, polite and exceptionally well constructed.

One day, while taking dictation she noticed that Mr.. Smith's fly was open and upon leaving the office, she said " Oh Mr.. Smith, did you know that the barracks door was open?"

He didn't understand her remark, but later noticed that his zipper was undone and decided to have some fun with his secretary.

He called her into his office. "By the way. Miss Jones, when you saw that the barracks door was open this morning, did you also see a soldier standing at attention?"

Although Miss Jones was young and polite, she was quite witty. She replied, "Why no, Mr.. Smith, all I saw was a disabled veteran sitting on an old duffle bag".

A chicken and an egg are lying in bed. The chicken is leaning against the headboard smoking a cigarette with a satisfied smile on its face.

The egg, looking a bit frustrated, grabs the sheet and rolls over and says, "Well, I guess we finally answered -THAT question!"

An 85 - year - old man marries a lovely 25 - year - old woman. Because her new husband is so old, the woman decides that on their wedding night they should have separate suites. She is concerned that the old fellow could over exert himself.

After the festivities she prepares herself for bed and for the knock on the door she is expecting. Sure enough the knock comes and there is her groom, ready for action.

They unite in conjugal union and all goes well, whereupon he takes his leave of her and she prepares to go to sleep for the night. A few minutes later, there's a knock on the door and there there stands the old guy - ready for more action. Somewhat surprised, she consents to further coupling, which is again successful, after which the octogenarian bids her a fond good night and leaves.

She is certainly ready for slumber at this point and is close to sleep for the second time when there is another knock at the door and there he is again, fresh as a 25 - year - old and ready for more. Once again they do it. As they're laying in the afterglow, the young bride says to him, "I am really impressed that a guy your age has enough energy to go for it three times. I've been with guys less than half your age that were only good for one."

The old guy looks puzzled and turns to her and says, "Was I already here?

A guy walks into a pharmacy and says to the pharmacist, "Listen, I have three girls coming over tonight. I've never had three girls at once, so I need something to keep me horny..... keep me potent."

The pharmacist reaches under the counter, unlocks the bottom drawer and takes out a small cardboard box marked with a label "Virile Extra Strength" and says, "Here, if you eat this, you'll go nuts for twelve hours. "

The guy says, "Gimme three boxes."

The next day the guy walks into the same pharmacy, limps up to the counter and pulls down his pants. The pharmacist looks in horror as he notices the man's penis is black and blue, and skin is hanging off in some places. In a pained voice, the man moans out, "Gimme a bottle of Deep Heat." The pharmacist replies in horror, "You can't put Deep Heat on that! " The man replies, "No, it's for my arms. The girls didn't show up."

Stan is ill one morning so he rings his boss and says, "Hey, boss I can't come to work today. I'm really sick. I've got a headache, stomach ache and my legs hurt, I can't come to work."

The boss says: "You know Stan, I really need you today. When I feel like this I go to my wife and tell her to give me some sex. That makes me feel better and I can go to work. You should try that."

Two hours later Stan calls: "Boss, I did what you said and I feel great, I'll be at work soon. By the way You've got a nice house."

Three desperately ill men met with their doctor one day to discuss their options. One was an alcoholic, one was a chain smoker and the other was a homosexual.

The doctor, addressing all three of them, said, "If any of you indulge in your vices one more time, you will surely die."

The men left the doctor's office, each convinced that he would never again indulge himself in his vice.

While walking toward the subway for their return trip to the suburbs, they passed a bar. The alcoholic, hearing the loud music and seeing the lights, could not stop himself.

His buddies accompanied him into the bar, where he had a shot of whisky.

No sooner had he replaced the shot glass on the bar, he fell off his stool, stone cold dead.

His companions, somewhat shaken, left the bar, realising how seriously they must take the words.

As they walked along, they came upon a cigarette butt lying on the ground, still burning. The homosexual looked at the chain smoker and said, "If you bend over to pick that up, we're both dead."

A brunette, a blonde and a redhead are all in year 9. Who has the biggest boobs?

The blonde, because she's 18

Pat comes to the pub one Monday with a shiner so black it looks like shoe polish. Mike looks him up and down, and says, "Mother Mary Pat, what happened to ye eye?" Mike says, "Well I was at Mass yesterday and I was sitting behind this enormous woman.

I swear to all the Saints she was as big as the Goodyear blimp in a dress! "Anyway, when she stood up to sing the hymn, I saw that the back of her dress was caught in the crack of her butt and I didn't want her to be embarrassed in front of the congregation, so I reached over and gave it a little tug, just to be helpful you know and with that she turned around and slugged me, you are seeing the result.

A week goes by.

The very next Monday, Pat shows up with the other eye all blackened.

Mike cocks his head and asks, "Alright now, how did ye get this one?"

Pat says "Well I was at Mass again yesterday,

and as fate would have it, I was sitting behind the very same enormous woman,

As we stood to sing the hymn, sure enough, the back of her dress was again caught in the crack of her butt."

Mike asked incredulously, "Don't tell me you did it again? Didn't you learn your lesson last week?"

Pat says "Oh no, not me, I'm not an idiot, ye know. I learned right enough and I wasn't going to touch that dress.

But you see the fellow sitting next to me reached over and tugged it out. Well I knew she didn't like people doing that, so... I reached over and tucked it back in...."

A man walking along the beach at Margate was deep in prayer.

Suddenly the clouds opened above his head and in a booming voice the Lord said, "Because you have TRIED to be faithful to me in all ways, I will grant you one wish."

The man said, "That's a good idea! Can you build me a bridge to France so that I can drive over and play golf anytime I like?"

The Lord said, "Hang on a sec, your request is very materialistic, and not too easy either. Think of the logistics: the supports required to reach the bottom of The Channel; the concrete and steel it would take! I can do it, but it's pretty hard to justify on any sensible cost: benefit basis, and I'm not sure that it would really be a good idea to satisfy such a worldly request. Why don't you take a little more time, think about it a bit more and maybe come up with a wish more worthy of both of us."

The man thought about it for a long time.

Finally he said, "Lord, I have been married and divorced four times. All of my wives said that I am uncaring and insensitive. I wish that I could understand women. I want to know how they feel inside, what they are thinking when they give me the silent treatment, why they cry, what they mean when they say 'nothing'. I would really like to be able to make just one woman truly happy."

After a few minutes God said,

"You want two lanes or four on that bridge?"

A guy goes to the local council to apply for a job.

The interviewer asks him "Have you been in the armed services ?"

"Yes" he says, "I was in Bosnia for three years."

The interviewer says "That will increase your chances of gaining employment".

He then asks, "Are you disabled in any way?"

The guy says "Yes 100%... a mortar round exploded near me and blew my testicles off."

The interviewer tells the guy "OK. I can hire you right now. The hours are 8.00 am to 4.00 pm. You can start tomorrow. Come in at 10.00 am..."

The guy is puzzled and says, "If the hours are from 8.00 am to 4.00 pm then why do you want me to come in at 10.00 am?"

"This is a council job" the interviewer replies. "For the first two hours we sit around scratching our balls. No point in you coming in for that."

There was this couple that were married for 20 years, and every time they had sex the husband always insisted on shutting off the lights.

Well, after 20 years the wife felt this was stupid. She figured she would break him out of the crazy habit.

So one night, while they were in the middle of doing it, she turned on the lights.

She looked down and saw her husband was holding a dildo.

She gets completely upset. "You impotent b*%#$£!d," she screamed at him, "how could you be lying to me all of these years? You better explain yourself!"

The husband looks her straight in the eyes and says, calmly, "I'll explain the dildo.......If you can explain our three kids."

Paul returned from a doctor's visit one day and told his wife Alma that the doctor said he only had 24 hours to live. Wiping away her tears, he asked her to make love with him. Of course she agreed and they made passionate love. Six hours later, Paul went to her again, and said, "Honey, now I only have 18 hours left to live. Maybe we could make love again? "Alma agrees-and again they make love. Later, Paul is getting into bed when he realised he now had only eight hours of life left. He touched Alma's shoulder and said, "Honey? Please? Just one more time before I die." She agreed, then afterward she rolled over and fell asleep. Paul, however, heard the clock ticking in his head, and he tossed and turned until he was down to only four more hours. He tapped his wife on the shoulder to wake her up. "Hon, I only have four hours left! Could we...?" His wife sat up abruptly, turned to him and said, "Listen Paul, I have to get up in the morning! You don't."

Three guys are talking in a bar. First guy says, "I was looking for a pen in my wife's handbag and found a bottle of gin. In 8 years of marriage I never knew she drank." Second guy says, "I recently found cigarettes in my wife's handbag, in 15 years I never knew she smoked." Third guy says, "Last night I found a packet of condoms in my wife's handbag. In 20 years of marriage I never knew she had a cock!"

A Frenchman, an Italian and an Englishman were discussing love-making.

"Last night I made love to my wife three times," boasted the Frenchman.

"She told me she was in sheer ecstasy this morning..."

"Ah, last night I made love to my wife six times," the Italian responded.

"This morning she made me a wonderful breakfast and told me she could never love any other man."

When the Englishman remained silent, the Frenchman smugly asked, "And how many times did you make love to your wife last night?"

"Once." he replied.

"Only once?" The Italian arrogantly snorted. "And what did she say to you this morning?"

"Don't stop."

Billy Bob and Luther were talking one afternoon when Billy Bob tells Luther, "Ya know, I reckon I'm 'bout ready for another vacation. Only this year I'm gonna do it a little different. The last few years, I took your advice about where to go. Three years ago you said, go to Hawaii. So I went to Hawaii and Earline got pregnant. Then, two years ago, you told me to go to the Bahamas, and Earline got pregnant again. Last year you suggested Tahiti and darned if Earline did - n - get pregnant again." Luther asks Billy Bob, "So, whacha gonna do different this year?" Billy Bob says, "This year I'm taking Earline with me."

A lady approaches her priest and says, "Father, I have a problem. I have two female talking parrots, but they only know how to say one thing."

"What do they say?" the priest inquires.

"They only know how to say, 'Hi, we're prostitutes. Want to have some fun?'"

"That's terrible," the priest exclaims, "but I have a solution to your problem. Bring your two female parrots over to my house, and I will put them with my two male talking parrots whom I taught to pray and read the bible. My parrots will teach your parrots to stop saying that terrible phrase, and your female parrots will learn to praise and worship."

"Thank you!" the woman responds.

The next day, the woman brings her female parrots to the priest's house. His two male parrots are holding rosary beads and praying in their cage. The lady puts her two female parrots in with the male parrots, and the female parrots say, "Hi, we're prostitutes, want to have some fun?"

One male parrot looks at the other male parrot and exclaims, "Put the beads away Francis our prayers have been answered!"

Why does Mike Tyson cry during sex?

Pepper spray will do that to you.

A professor at the University is giving a seminar on the supernatural.

To get a feel for his audience, he asks them, "How many folk here believe in ghosts?"

About 80 students raise their hands.

"That's a good start," says the professor, "For those who believe in ghosts, do any of you think you've ever seen a ghost?"

About 40 students raise their hands.

"That's really good," continues the professor, "I'm really glad you take this seriously.

Has anyone here ever talked to a ghost?"

15 students raise their hands.

"That's a great response," remarks the impressed professor, "has anyone here ever touched a ghost?" 3 students raise their hands.

"Brilliant. But let me ask you one question further...

Have any of you ever been intimate with a ghost?"

One of his students from the country raises his

hand.

The professor is astonished. He takes off glasses, takes a step back, and says, "Son, all the years I've been giving this lecture, no one has ever claimed that. You've got to come up here and tell us about your experience".

The redneck student replies with a nod and begins to make his way up to the podium.

The professor asks, "Well, tell us what it's like to have made love to a ghost."

The student replies. "Ghost?!? Damn!... I thought you said 'goats.'

An extraordinarily handsome man decided he had the God-given responsibility to marry the perfect woman so they could produce children beyond comparison. With that as his mission he began searching for the perfect woman. After a diligent, but fruitless, search up and down the east coast, he started to head west. Shortly thereafter he met a farmer who had three stunning, gorgeous daughters that positively took his breath away. So he explained his mission to the farmer, asking for permission to marry one of them.

The farmer simply replied, "They're all lookin" to get married, so you came to the right place. Look them over and select the one you want." The man dated the first daughter. The next day the farmer asked for the man's opinion. "Well" said the man," She's just a weeeeee bit, not that you can hardly notice, but pigeon-toed."

The farmer nodded and suggested the man date one of the other girls; so the man went out with the second daughter. The next day, the farmer again asked how things went. "Well," the man replied, "She's just a weeeee bit, not that you can hardly tell, cross-eyed."

The farmer nodded and suggested he date the third girl to see if things might be better. So he did. The next morning the man rushed in exclaiming, "She's perfect, just perfect! She's the one I want to marry!" So they were wed right away.

Months later the baby was born. When the man visited the nursery he was horrified: the baby was the ugliest, most pathetic human you can imagine.

He rushed to his father-in-law asking how such a thing could happen considering the parents. "Well," explained the farmer, "She was just a weeeee bit, not that you could hardly tell pregnant when you met her."

The mother-in-law stopped unexpectedly by the recently married couple's house.

She rang the doorbell and stepped into the house.

She saw her daughter-in-law standing naked by the door.

"What are you doing?" she asked.

"I'm waiting for my husband to come home from work," the daughter-in-law answered.

"But you're naked!" the mother - in - law exclaimed.

"This is my love dress," the daughter-in-law explained.

"Love dress? But you're naked!"

"My husband loves me to wear this dress! It makes him happy and it makes me happy. I would appreciate it if you would leave because he will be home from work any minute."

The mother-in-law was tired of all this romantic talk and left.

On the way home she thought about the love

dress. When she got home she
undressed, showered, put on her best perfume
and waited by the front door.

Finally her husband came home. He walked in
and saw her standing naked by the door.

"What are you doing?" he asked.

"This is my love dress" she replied.

'Needs ironing." he said as he brushed past
her.

He said... I don't know why you wear a bra you've got nothing to put in it.

She said... You wear briefs, don't you?

Why do men find it difficult to make eye contact?

Breasts don't have eyes.

An exquisite painting entitled "Home for Lunch" was on display in a Cardiff art gallery. It depicted three very naked, very black men sitting on a park bench. What was unusual was that the men on both ends of the bench had black penises, but the man in the middle had a very pink penis.

Two women were staring at the painting, trying to figure it out. The artist noticed their confusion. The artist asked, "Can I help you with this painting?"

One woman replied, "We were curious about the painting of the black men on the bench. Why does the man in the middle have a pink penis?"

"I'm afraid you've misinterpreted the painting," the artist explained. "The three men are not African-Caribbean. They are Welsh coal miners, and the fellow in the middle went home for lunch."

What is the difference between a Harley and a Hoover.

The position of the dirtbag

What's the difference between a northern USA fairytale and a southern USA fairytale?

A northern fairytale begins 'Once upon a time...' A southern fairytale begins 'Y'all ain't gonna believe this shit...'

A teacher notices that a little boy at the back of the class is squirming around, scratching his crotch and not paying attention. She went to the back to find out what was going on. He was quite embarrassed and whispered that he had just recently been circumcised and was quite itchy.

The teacher told him to go to the head teacher's office and phone his mother for advice.

He did, and returned to his classroom and resumed his seat. Suddenly, there was a commotion at the back of the room. The teacher went to investigate only to find him sitting at his desk with his penis hanging out.

"I thought I told you to call your mother for advice." she screamed. "I did," he said, "and she told me that if I could stick it out till lunch break, she'd come and pick me up."

A man, who smelled like a distillery, flopped down on a park seat next to a priest. The man's tie was stained, his face was plastered in lipstick and a half empty bottle of vodka was sticking out of his shabby jacket pocket. He opened his news paper and began reading. After a few minutes the dishevelled man turned to the priest and said "Father, what causes arthritis?" "Mister, it's caused by loose living, being with wicked women, alcohol abuse and contempt for your fellow man."

"Well I'll be damned," the drunk muttered, returning to his paper.

The priest, thinking on what he had said, nudged the man and apologised. "I'm very sorry, I didn't mean to come on so strong. How long have you had arthritis?" "I don't have it Father," said the man, "I was just reading that the Pope does."

He said... 'Two inches more, and I would be king'

She said... 'Two inches less, and you would be queen.'

He said... "Shall we try a different position tonight?"

She said... "That's a good idea.... you stand by the ironing board while I sit on the sofa and fart."

A man met a beautiful lady and decided he wanted to marry her right away.

She said, "But we don't know anything about each other." He said, "That's all right, we'll learn about each other as we go along." She consented, they were married and went on honeymoon to a very nice resort.

One morning they were lying by the pool when he got up off his towel, climbed up to the 10 metre board an did a two and a half tuck gainer followed by three rotations in the jackknife position, where he straightened out and cut the water like a knife.

After a few more demonstrations, he came back and lay on the towel. She said, "That was incredible!." He said, "I used to be an Olympic diving champion. You see, I told you we'd learn more about ourselves as we went along." She got up, jumped into the pool and started to do laps.

After about 30 laps, she climbed out and lay

on her towel hardly out of breath. He said, "That was incredible! were you an Olympic endurance swimmer?" "No," she said, "I was a hooker in Venice and I worked both sides of the canal."

What would you call it when an Italian has one arm shorter than the other?

A speech impediment.

When I was 14, I hoped that one day I would have a girlfriend.

When I was 16 I got a girlfriend, but there was no passion. So I decided I needed a passionate girl with a zest for life.

In college I dated a passionate girl, but she was too emotional. Everything was an emergency, she was a drama queen, cried all the time and threatened suicide. So I decided I needed a girl with some stability.

When I was 25 I found a very stable girl but she was boring. She was totally predictable and never got excited about anything. Life became so dull that I decided I needed a girl with some excitement.

When I was 28 I found an exciting girl, but I couldn't keep up with her. She rushed from one thing to another, never settling on anything. She did mad impetuous things and flirted with everyone she met. She made me miserable as often as happy. She was great fun initially and very energetic, but directionless. So I decided to find a girl with some ambition. When I turned 31, I found a smart ambitious girl with her feet planted firmly on the ground and married her. She was so ambitious that she divorced me and took everything I owned. Now I am 40 and all I want is a girl with big boobs.

What's the fastest way to a man's heart?

Through the chest with a sharp knife.

Three couples, an elderly couple, a middle-aged couple and a young newlywed couple wanted to join a church.

The Vicar said, "We have special requirements for new parishioners. You must abstain from having sex for two weeks."

The couples agreed and came back at the end of two weeks.

The Vicar went to the elderly couple and asked, "Were you able to abstain from sex for the two weeks?"

The old man replied, "No problem at all Vicar."

"Congratulations! Welcome to the church!" said the Vicar.

The Vicar went to the middle-aged couple and asked, "Well, were you able to abstain from sex for the two weeks?"

The man replied, "The first week was not too bad. The second week I had to sleep on the couch for a couple of nights but, yes we made it."

"Congratulations! Welcome to the church!" said the Vicar.

The Vicar went to the newlywed couple and asked, "Well, were you able to abstain from sex for two weeks?"

"No Vicar, we were not able to go without sex for the two weeks," the young man replied sadly. "What Happened?" inquired the Vicar.

"My wife was reaching for a can of corn on the top shelf and dropped it. When she bent over to pick it up, I was overcome with lust and took advantage of her right there."

"You understand, of course, this means you will not be welcome in our church," stated the Vicar.

"We Know." said the young man, "We're not welcome at the local supermarket anymore either.'

A married couple sleepily awoke one Saturday morning.

The wife rolled over and inquired, "Are you going to mow the lawns today?"

The husband replied, "Who do I look like - Alan Titchmarsh?"

Not being quick to give up, she continued, "How about mending the TV aerial then?"

"Who do I look like The TV Man?" He sarcastically replied again.

She sighed, and he got up and went off to his golf game.

When he returned home, the aerial was fixed and the lawn mowed.

"Who the hell did this?" The husband asked, flabbergasted.

"The TV Man and Alan Titchmarsh," the wife replied, smiling smugly.

"How did you afford it?" The husband inquired, becoming nervous.

"Well, they said I could either bake them each a

pie or make love to them," said the wife.

"So what sort of pies did you bake?" the husband continued, a little more relieved.

The wife replied, "Who do I look like - Delia Smith?

He said... Why don't you tell me when you have an orgasm?

She said... I would, but you're never there

A kindergarten class had a homework assignment to find out about something exciting and relate it to the class the next day.

When the time came to present what they'd found, the first little boy called upon walked up to the front of the class, and with a piece of chalk, made a small white dot on the blackboard, then sat back down.

Puzzled, the teacher asked him just what it was. "It's a period," said the little boy. "Well, I can see that," she said, "but what is so exciting about a period?"

"Damned if I know," said the little boy," but this morning my sister was missing one, Dad went crazy, Mummy fainted, and our next door neighbour left town".

There are these two statues in a park; one of a nude man and one of a nude woman.

They had been facing each other across a pathway for a hundred years, when one day an angel comes down from the sky and, with a single gesture, brings the two to life.

The angel tells them, "As a reward for being so patient through a hundred blazing summers and dismal winters, you have been given life for thirty minutes to do what you've wished to do the most. "He looks at her, she looks at him, and they go running behind the shrubbery.

The angel waits patiently as the bushes rustle and giggling ensues.

After fifteen minutes, the two return, out of breath and laughing. The angel tells them, "Urn, you have fifteen minutes left. Would you care to do it again?" He asks her, "Shall we?" She eagerly replies, "Oh, yes, let's!... But let's change positions. This time I hold the pigeon down and you crap on its head!"

A man and a woman had been dating for a while. The woman was modest and held back on her virtues.

The man had never even seen her naked.

One day while driving out in the country she remarked about his slow driving habits.

"I can't stand this" she told him.

"Let's play a game. For every 5 miles per hour you go over the speed limit, I'll remove a piece of my clothes."

He happily agreed and sped up to 55- so she took off her blouse- at 60 off came the skirt-at 65 her bra and at 70 her panties.

Now seeing her naked for the first time and travelling faster than he ever had before, he lost control of the car, went off the road and hit a tree.

His girlfriend wasn't hurt but he was trapped.

She tried to pull him out but he was stuck! "Go to the road and get help" he said.

"But I don't have anything to cover myself with"

she replied.

The man felt around, but could only find 1 of his shoes.

"Just put this between your legs to cover it up" he told her.

So she did as he said and went up to the road for help.

Along came a truck driver and seeing a naked hysterical woman, he pulled over to see what was wrong.

"My boyfriend", "My boyfriend" she sobbed. He's stuck and I can't get him out!

The truck driver, looking down at the shoe between her legs, replies "Maam, if he's in that far, I'm afraid he's a goner!

S ister Margaret had been a model nun all her life, but then she was called "to her reward."

As she approached the Pearly Gates, Saint Peter said "Hold on. Sister Margaret... not so fast!" "But I have been good all my life and dedicated to the work of the Lord. From the time I was taken in as an infant by the sisters at the convent, to my dying breath ... I have lived for this moment!" Sister Margaret exclaimed in disbelief. "That is just the problem... you never learned right from wrong and to get into heaven, you must know the difference between right and wrong," replied St. Peter. "Well, what can I do? I will do anything to get into heaven," Sister Margaret pleaded. "I am going to have to send you back down to Earth. When you get there, I want you to smoke a cigarette and call me when you are finished—we will discuss your situation then," ordered St. Peter.

Sister Margaret returned to Earth, smoked a

Camel, and then called St. Peter coughing and hacking. "Saint Peter" she gasped, "I can hardly breathe ... my mouth tastes terrible, my breath stinks, I feel dizzy, and I think I am going to throw up!" "Good!" replied the old saint, "Now you are finally getting a feel for right and wrong. Now go out tonight and drink some hard liquor and call me immediately."

Sister Margaret phoned St. Peter shortly after taking several belts of Whisky.

"Saint Peter... I feel woozy that vile liquid burned my throat and nauseated me ... it is all I can do to keep it down." "Good—good! Now you ore starting to see the difference between right and wrong" said St. Peter with delight. "Tomorrow I want you to seek out a man and "know him" in the Biblical sense, then call me "A week later. Sister Margaret called St. Peter and left a message. "Hello, Pete it's Maggy It's gonna be a while!"

A lonely spinster, aged 70, decided that it was time to get married.

She decided to put an ad in the local paper that read: "HUSBAND WANTED, must be in my age group, must not beat me, must not run around on me, and must still be good in bed!

All applicants apply in person."

On the second day she heard the doorbell. Much to her dismay she opened the door to see a gray haired gentleman sitting in a wheel chair. He had no arms or legs.

She asked sardonically, "You're not really asking me to consider you, are you? Just look at you... you have no legs!"

The old man smiled, "Therefore I cannot run around on you!"

She snorted, "You don't have any hands either!"

Again the old man smiled, "Nor can I beat you!"

She raised an eyebrow and gazed intently, "Are

you still good in bed?"
With that, the old gentleman beamed a broad smile, "I rang the doorbell didn't I?"

Two elderly ladies are sitting on the front porch, doing nothing.
One lady turns and asks, "Do you still get horny?"
"Oh sure I do. The second lady replies, "I suck a life saver."
After a few moments, the first lady asks, "Who drives you to the beach?

In The Garden of Eden God said, "Go down into that valley." Adam said, "What's a valley? "God explained it to him. Then God said, "Cross the river. "Adam said "What's a river?" and God explained that to him too. Then God said, "Go over the hill." Adam said, "What's a hill?" Again, God explained it to him. Then God told Adam, "On the other side of the hill, you will find a cave." Adam said, "What's a cave?" and God explained that to him. "In the cave you will find a woman." Adam said, "What's a woman?" So God explained that to him, and said. "I want you to reproduce." Adam said, "How do I do that?" So God explained it to him. So off went Adam, down into the valley, across the river, and over the hill, and into the cave. and found the woman, and in about five minutes he was back. God said angrily, "What is it now?"

Adam asked, "What's a headache?"

An old woman and old man are sitting on the porch one evening rocking in their rocking chairs.

Out of the blue the old woman reaches over and whacks the old man in the head and he falls out of the chair and down the steps.

He gets up slowly and says what the heck did you do that for you old fool? The old woman replies "That's for 60 years of bad sex!"

So the old man sits down and they continue rocking. Then the old man reaches over whacks the old lady and she rolls out of the chair and down the steps. She gets up and asks, "What the heck was that for?" The old man says, "That's for knowing the difference."

This guy went to the zoo one day. While he was standing in front of the gorilla's enclosure, the wind gusted and he got some grit in his eye. As he pulled his eyelid down to dislodge the particle, the gorilla went crazy, bent open the bars, and beat the guy senseless.

When the guy came to, the zoo keeper was anxiously bending over him. As soon as he was able to talk, he explained what had happened. The zoo keeper nodded and explained that in gorilla language, pulling down your eyelid means, "F*ck you. "This didn't make the gorilla's victim feel any better and he vowed revenge. The next day he purchased two large knives, two party hats, two party horns, and a large sausage. Putting the sausage in his pants, he hurried to the zoo and over to the gorilla's cage, into which he tossed a hat, a knife, and a party horn.

Knowing that the big apes were natural mimics,

he put on a party hat.

The gorilla looked at him, and looked at the hat, and put it on. Next he picked up his horn and blew on it. The gorilla picked up his horn and did the same. Then the man picked up his knife, whipped the sausage out of his pants, and sliced it neatly in two. The gorilla looked at the knife in his cage, looked at his own crotch, and pulled down his eyelid.

An old man was sitting on a bench at the mall. A young man walked up to the bench and sat down. He had spiked hair in all different colours: green, red, orange, blue, and yellow. The old man just stared. The young man said sarcastically, "What's the matter old timer, never done anything wild in your life?"

Without batting an eye, the old man replied, "Got drunk once and had sex with a parrot. I was just wondering if you were my son."

The preacher was preaching with all his might. The subject was SIN, and he was most certainly 'against' it.

A girl, with a wonderful figure, and not nearly enough clothes to hide much skin, came in late. She strode down the centre aisle, close to the front, and sat down.

It was plain to the preacher that he had lost the men in his audience to this voluptuous sex-object.

He shook a fist at her and said, "You are the Jezebel the good book tells us about. You have got the mind of every man in this building on evil thoughts and not good thoughts. But I am a man of God! You don't affect me, and right now up in Heaven, Saint Finger is shaking his Peter at you!!"

Doctor Bob had slept with one of his patients and had felt guilty all day long.

No matter how much he tried to forget about it, he couldn't.

The guilt and sense of betrayal was overwhelming.

But every once in a while he'd hear that soothing voice, within himself, trying to reassure him.

"Bob, don't worry about it. You aren't the first doctor to sleep with one of their patients and you won't be the last. And you're single. Let it go...." Just let it go.........

But invariably the other voice would bring him back to reality "Bob, it would whisper quite distinctly you're a Vet...."

A man walks into a bar in Arkansas and orders a white wine. Everyone in the bar looked up very surprised. The bartender looked at the man stating, "Your not from around here are you." "No sir, I'm from Iowa." The bartender then asked, "what do you do in Iowa." "I'm a taxidermist." "A taxidermist, now what heck is that." The man said "I mount animals" The bartender smiles and shouts out, "It's OK boys he one of us.."

Mr. Smith owned a small business. He had two employees, Sarah and Jack. They were both extremely good employees always willing to work overtime and chip in where needed. Mr. Smith was looking over his books one day and decided that he wasn't making enough money to warrant two employees and he would have to lay one off. But both Sarah and Jack were such good workers he was having trouble finding a fair way to do it.

He decided that he would watch them work and the first one to take a break would be the one he would lay off. So, he sat in his office and watched them work.

Suddenly, Sarah gets a terrible headache and needs to take an aspirin. She gets the aspirin out of her purse and goes to the water cooler to get something to wash it down with.

Mr. Smith follows her to the water cooler, taps her on the shoulder and says, "Sarah. I'm going to have to lay you or Jack off."

And Sarah says, "Can you jack off? I have a headache!".

A young attractive women leaves the bar to go to the bathroom and momentarily returns. She goes up to the bartender, and gets his attention. She then begins talking to him, stroking her fingers along his long sleeved shirt up to his shoulders and collar. She begins asking if he was the manager, he replies "No" As she runs her fingers through his beard, in a seductive manner she asks him to deliver a message to the manager. As he awaits for the message she slips her fingers into his mouth, and he begins sucking on them. She tells him: "Tell your manager that there is no toilet paper in the ladies .."

A woman went to a pet shop and immediately spotted a large beautiful parrot.

There was a sign on the cage that said £50.00.

"Why so little," she asked the pet store owner.

The owner looked at her and said, "Look, I should tell you first that this bird used to live in a house of prostitution, and sometimes it says some pretty vulgar stuff."

The woman thought about this, but decided she had to have the bird anyway.

She took it home and hung the bird's cage up in her living room and waited for it to say something.

The bird looked around the room, then at her, and said, "New house, new madam."

The woman was a bit shocked at the implication, but then thought "that's not so bad."

When her two teenage daughters returned from school the bird saw them and said, "New house, new madam, new girls".

The girls and the woman were a bit offended but then began to laugh about the situation. Moments later, the woman's husband, Keith, came home from work
The bird looked at him and said, "Hi Keith"

What do lawyers use for birth control?

Their personalities

An American touring Spain stopped at a local restaurant following a day of sightseeing. While sipping his sangria, he noticed a sizzling, scrumptious looking platter being served at the next table. Not only did it look good the smell was wonderful. He asked the waiter. "What is that you just served?"

The waiter replied, "Ah senor, you have excellent taste! Those are bulls testicles from the bull fight this morning. A delicacy!"

The American, though momentarily daunted, said, "What the hell, I'm on vacation! Bring me an order!" The waiter replied, "I am so sorry senor. There is only one serving per day because there is only one bull fight each morning. If you come early tomorrow and place your order, we will be sure to save you this delicacy!"

The next morning, the American returned, placed his order, and then that evening he was served the one and only special delicacy of the day. After a few bites, and enjoying the delicacies of his platter, he called to the waiter and said, "These are delicious, but they are much, much smaller portions than the ones I saw you serve yesterday! I did pay for a full serving did I not?" The waiter shrugged his shoulders and replied, "Si senor. Sometimes the bull wins."

What's the difference between a boyfriend and husband?

About 45 minutes.

A man went into a pharmacy and asked to talk to a male pharmacist.

The woman he was talking to said that she was the pharmacist and that she and her sister owned the store, so there were no males employed there. She then asked if there was something which she could help the gentleman with. The man said that it was something that he would be much more comfortable discussing with a male pharmacist. The female pharmacist assured him that she was completely professional and whatever it was that he needed to discuss, he could be confident that she would treat him with the highest level of professionalism. The man agreed and began by saying, "This is tough for me to discuss, but I have a permanent erection. It causes me a lot of problems and severe embarrassment. So I was wondering what you could give me for it?"

The pharmacist said, "Just a minute, I'll go talk to my sister." When she returned, she said,

"We discussed it at length and the absolute best we can do is, 1/3 ownership in the store, a company car, and £3000 a month living expenses."

Why do men want to marry virgins?

They can't stand the criticism.

An older man marries a younger lady and they are very much in love.

However, no matter what the husband does sexually, the woman never achieves orgasm. In order to make the marriage "better", they decide to ask their priest for help.

The priest listens to their story. "I have the solution. Hire a strapping young man. While the two of you are making love, have the young man wave a towel over you. That will help the wife fantasise and should bring on an orgasm."

The couple go home and follow the priest's advice. They hire a handsome young man and he waves a towel over them as they make love. But it doesn't help and she is still unsatisfied. Perplexed, they go back to the priest. "Ahh," says the priest to the husband, "try it reversed. Have the young man make love to your wife and you wave the towel over them."

Once again, they follow the priest's advice.

The young man gets into bed with the wife

and the husband waves the towel. The young man gets to work with great enthusiasm and the wife soon has an enormous, room-shaking, screaming orgasm. The husband smiles, and looks at the young man "See? THAT'S how you were supposed to wave the towel."

Why is it so hard for women to find men that are sensitive, caring, and good-looking?

Because those men already have boyfriends.

Two elderly gentlemen, who had been without sex for several years, decided they needed to visit a whore house.

When they arrived at the house, the Madame took one look at them and decided she wasn't going to waste any of her girls on these two old men. So she used "blow-up" dolls instead.

She put the dolls in each man's room and left them to their business.

After the two men were finished, they started for home and got to talking.

The first man said, "I think the girl I had was dead. She never moved, talked, or groaned.... how was it for you?" The second man replied, "I think mine was a witch." The first man asked. "How's that?" "Well," said the second man, "when I nibbled on her breast... she just farted and flew out the window!"

Hillary Clinton died and went to heaven. As she stood in front of St. Peter at the Pearly Gates she saw a huge wall of clocks behind him.

She asked, "What are all those clocks?"

St. Peter replied, "Those are Lie-Clocks. Everyone on Earth has a Lie-Clock. Every time you lie the hands on your clock will move."

"Oh," said Hillary, "whose clock is that?"

"That's Mother Teresa's. The hands have never moved indicating that she never told lie."

"Whose clock is that?"

"That's Abraham Lincoln's clock. The hands have only moved twice telling us that Abe only told 2 lies in his entire life."

"Where's Bill's clock?" Hillary asked.

"Bill's clock is in Jesus' office. He's using it as a ceiling fan."

A very confident James Bond walks into a bar and takes a seat next to a very attractive woman.

He gives her a quick glance, then casually looks at his watch for a moment.

The women notices this and asks, "Is your date running late?"

"No", he replies, "Q's Just given me this state-of-the-art watch and I was just testing it."

The intrigued woman says, "A state-of-the-art watch? What's so special about it?"

Bond explains, "It uses alpha waves to talk to me telepathically."

The lady says, "what's it telling you now?"

"Well, it says you're not wearing any panties...."

The woman giggles and replies, "Well it must be broken because I am wearing panties!"

Bond shrugs, taps his watch and says, "Damn things an hour fast."

A woman is helping her computer-illiterate husband set up his computer.

She tells him that he will now need to choose and enter a password - something he will remember to log on.

The husband is in a rather amorous mood and figures he will try for the shock effect to bring this to his wife's attention.

So, when the computer asks him to enter a password, he makes it plainly obvious to his wife that he is keying in "penis".....

His wife nearly falls off her chair from laughing when the computer replies:

PASSWORD REJECTED. NOT LONG

ENOUGH

Three nuns passed every day through a street that led them from Church to a Reformatory. They noticed a parrot that stood at the entrance of a big residential house. Every time they passed in front of that house, the bird would pronounce three sequential colours.

One day, they heard "yellow, blue, black." One of the nuns noticed that those colours perfectly matched the colour of their underwear. She mentioned her discovery to the other two nuns, but both were reluctant to believe that could be possible.

The next day, they all wore black underwear and passed in front of the house, and very precisely the parrot spoke, "black, black, black." Hearing that, the three nuns were astonished!!. One of the nuns spoke up: "Girls, tomorrow we are going to trick that bird."

Saying that, she recommended that the next day, none of them should wear any underwear under their vestments. Respecting their agreement, next day they wore no underwear and proceeded to pass in front of the parrot's house.

They peeked at the bird. At the beginning, the parrot looked a bit puzzled, he swung back and forth on the cane he was perched on.

Then, after a while, the Parrot spoke: "Straight, Straight, Curly!"

What do you get if you put 50 lesbians and 50 politicians in a room together?

100 people who don't do dick.

A man and a woman who have never met before find themselves in the same sleeping carriage of a train.

After the initial embarrassment, they both manage to get to sleep, the woman on the top bunk, the man on the lower.

In the middle of the night, the woman leans over and says, "I'm sorry to bother you, but I'm awfully cold and I was wondering if you could possibly pass me another blanket."

The man leans out and, with a glint in his eye, says, "I've got a better idea.... let's pretend we're married."

"Why not," giggles the woman.

"Good", he replies. "Get your own f*cking blanket."

An old country doctor went way out onto the fells to deliver a baby.

It was so far out, there was no electricity. When the doctor arrived, no one was home except for the labouring mother and her 5-year-old child.

The doctor instructed the child to hold a lantern high so he could see, while he helped the woman deliver the baby.

The child did so.

The mother pushed and after a little while, the doctor lifted the newborn baby by the feet and spanked him on the bottom to get him to take his first breath.

The doctor then asked the 5-year-old what he thought of the baby.

"Spank him again," the 5-year-old said. "He shouldn't have crawled in there in the first place."

A wealthy couple had plans to go to an evening ball so they advised their butler that they were giving him the night off to do as he pleases as they would be late home.

The couple went to the ball but after a while the wife told her husband she was bored and could they go home.

The husband responded that he needed to stay longer to entertain some business friends.

So the wife went home alone and found the butler spread out on the sofa watching TV.

She slowly moved towards him and sat down very seductively.

She then told him to come closer, then even closer. She moved towards him and whispered in his ear, "Take off my dress."

"Now take off my bra." "Now take off my shoes and stockings and remove my panties."

She then looked deep into his eyes and said "Next time I catch you wearing my clothes, you're fired."

An Englishman, an Irishman and a Scotsman go into a pub. They all suffer from a severe stutter. "What's it to be?" asks the stunningly beautiful landlady. "Th th th three pi pi pi .." says the Englishman.

Up steps the Irishman. "Threeee p pints of of of of gui gui gui gui................."

Then the Scotsman tries. "Th th th thth th th th th th th th th th................."

"Oh bugger this!" says the beautiful landlady and walks away to serve someone else.

She returns ten minutes later and asks if they are ready to order yet.

"Th th th three pi pi ", stutters the Englishman.

"Three pints of gui gui gui gui....." tries Paddy.

And then Scotty starts "Th th th th th ....".

"Look" says the beautiful landlady, who loves a bet, "If any one of you can answer a question without stuttering I'll let you shag me!" Quite confident that no one will win, she turns to the Englishman. "Where do you live?" "M M M M

Man Man Man Manch Manch Manch." "No. You lose." says the beautiful landlady. Turning to the Scotsman, she asks, "Where do you live Scotty?", trying not to laugh. "E E E Ed Ed Ed Edin Edin Edin Edinb." "Sorry, you lose." says the gorgeous woman. "And Paddy, where do you live?" she purrs at the Irishman. "London" blurts out the Irishman. "Oh. Bugger!" says the landlady. A great cheer goes up in the pub and the landlady reluctantly takes him by the hand and leads him upstairs.

Once in the bedroom she strips to her underwear, next she takes off her bra exposing a voluptuous bosom. Finally she slides off her panties then climbs into bed.

Paddy with concentration climbs aboard and goes for glory, and then, right at the climaxing stroke, he suddenly screams out " " "............- D D D Derry!!"

An angry wife met her husband at the door. There was alcohol on his breath and lipstick on his collar.

"I assume," she snarled, "that there is a very good reason for you to come waltzing in here at six o'clock in the morning?"

"There is," he replied. "Breakfast."

A man was washed up on a beach after a terrible shipwreck. Only a sheep and a sheepdog were washed up with him. After looking around, he realised that they were stranded on a deserted island.

After being there awhile, he got into the habit of taking his two animal companions to the beach every evening to watch the sunset.

On particular evening, the sky was a fiery red with beautiful cirrus clouds, the breeze was warm and gentle — a perfect night for romance.

As they sat there, the sheep started looking better and better to the lonely man. Soon, he leaned over to the sheep and put his arm around it.

But the sheepdog, ever protective of the sheep growled fiercely until the man took his arm from around the sheep.

After that, the three of them continued to enjoy the sunsets together, but there was no more cuddling.

A few weeks passed by and, lo and behold, there was another shipwreck.

The only survivor was Hillary Clinton.

That evening, the man brought Hillary to the evening beach ritual. It was another beautiful evening — red sky, cirrus clouds, a warm and gentle breeze — perfect for a night of romance. Pretty soon, the man started to get 'those feelings' again...

He fought the urges as long as he could but he finally gave in and leaned over to Hillary and told her he hadn't had sex for months.

Hillary batted her eyelashes and asked if there was anything she could do for him.

He said "Would you mind taking the dog for a walk?"

How do you get a sweet little 80 year old lady to say the F...word?

Get another sweet little 80 year old lady to yell *BINGO*!

What did the blonde say when she found out she was pregnant?

"Are you sure it's mine?"